D0847733

Getting Started with REBT

Rational Emotive Behaviour Therapy (REBT) encourages direct focus on emotional problems, encouraging understanding of the thoughts, beliefs and behaviour that are responsible for maintaining these problems. REBT encourages a healthier outlook by teaching individuals to challenge their irrational thoughts.

Getting Started with REBT provides a concise guide to assessing the suitability of REBT and using this method to address your emotional problems. The book is divided into two sections, beginning with an introduction to the theory and practice of REBT that will enable the reader to make an informed decision about whether this method is right for them. The second section guides the reader through issues that are relevant to all emotional problems, demonstrating how to:

- Formulate emotional problems and set goals
- Question irrational and rational beliefs
- Strengthen conviction in rational beliefs

Getting Started with REBT is suitable for use either alone or in conjunction with work with an REBT therapist. It will also be of interest to therapists and counsellors.

Windy Dryden is an REBT therapist and a Professor of Psychotherapeutic Studies at Goldsmiths College, London

GETTING STARTED WITH REBT

A Concise Guide for Clients

Windy Dryden

Routledge
Taylor & Francis Group

LONDON AND NEW YORK

First published 2006 by Routledge
27 Church Road, Hove, East Sussex, BN3 2FA

Simultaneously published in the USA and Canada
by Routledge
270 Madison Avenue, New York, NY10016

*Routledge is an imprint of the Taylor & Francis Group,
an informa business*

© 2006 Windy Dryden

Typeset in LucidaCasual
by Keystroke, 28 High Street, Tettenhall, Wolverhampton
Printed and bound in Great Britain
by TJ International Ltd, Padstow, Cornwall
Paperback cover design by Anú Design

This publication has been produced with paper manufactured
to strict environmental standards and with pulp derived from
sustainable forests.

British Library Cataloguing in Publication Data
A catalogue record for this book is available from the British Library

Library of Congress Cataloging in Publication Data
Dryden, Windy.
    Getting started with REBT : a concise guide for clients / by Windy
Dryden.
      p. ; cm.
      Includes bibliographical references and index.
    ISBN-13: 978-1-58391-938-5 (hbk)
    ISBN-10: 1-58391-938-4 (hbk)
    ISBN-13: 978-1-58391-939-2 (pbk)
    ISBN-10: 1-58391-939-2 (pbk)
    1. Rational emotive behavior therapy-Popular works. 2. Rational
    emotive behavior therapy-Handbooks, manuals, etc. I. Title. II. Title:
    Getting started with rational emotive behavior therapy.
    [DNLM: 1. Psychotherapy, Rational-Emotive-Handbooks. 2.
Psychotherapy, Rational-Emotive-Popular Works. WM 34 D799g 2006]

    RC489.R3D7867 2006
    616.89′14-dc22

ISBN13: 978-1-58391-938-5 (hbk)
ISBN13: 978-1-58391-939-2 (pbk)

ISBN10: 1-58391-938-4 (hbk)
ISBN10: 1-58391-939-2 (pbk)

Contents

Introduction

In 2001, I published a client workbook entitled *Reason to Change*. This book is a systematic, detailed, step-by-step guide to Rational Emotive Behaviour Therapy (REBT) that you can use on your own or with an REBT therapist. While this book was well received by clients and practitioners alike, I decided to write the present book in response to two pieces of recurring feedback. First, many clients who found the workbook valuable wanted a more portable version. This group argued that the workbook was too unwieldy to carry around and asked me to write a short version which retained the essence of the workbook, but which was far less detailed. Second, a number of clients said that they did not have time to go through the workbook and urged me to write a much shorter version. Echoing the first group, these clients wanted a book which retained the essence of the workbook, but was much shorter.

So here in response to popular demand is such a book. It will, in succinct terms, help you to understand what REBT is so that you can judge, from an informed position, whether or not it is for you. And if REBT is for you, it will help you get started in using the basic framework and methods of REBT to address your emotional problems. You can use this book on your own or in your work with an REBT therapist. In particular, I recommend that you consult an REBT therapist if your problems are quite complex or if you get stuck using this book and/or the workbook from which it is derived.

I hope you find this book valuable. Also, I encourage you to write to me c/o the publisher and let me know of your experiences in using it and your suggestions for improvement.

PART 1

Preparing You to Give Informed Consent

Psychological therapy is an ethical enterprise and whether you are using this book on your own or while consulting an REBT therapist, it is important that you give your informed consent to proceed with therapy using REBT. Before you give your consent to proceed, it is important that you are informed about the basics of REBT theory and practice. What I will do in this part of the book is to provide you with basic information about REBT: about how it sheds light on your emotional problems and about how it goes about helping you to address your problems. At the end of my presentation, you should have sufficient information about REBT to make an informed judgement concerning its utility in helping you deal with your emotional problems.

I

The Theory of Rational Emotive Behaviour Therapy

The theory of REBT has a number of features and it is important that you understand what these are before you commit yourself to using REBT either as a self-help therapy or with an REBT therapist.

1

How REBT Makes Sense of Emotional Problems and the Healthy Alternatives to these Problems

All approaches to counselling and psychotherapy have their own framework for making sense of people's emotional problems and the healthy alternatives to these problems, and REBT is no exception. In this section, I will discuss how REBT makes sense of *both* common emotional problems *and* healthy alternatives to these problems. My purpose in doing so, as I have noted above, is to help you make an informed judgement concerning whether or not REBT is for you.

THE REBT VIEW OF EMOTIONAL PROBLEMS

REBT is one of the cognitive-behavioural approaches to counselling and psychotherapy. As such, it particularly, but not exclusively, focuses on what you think and how you act as ways of helping you to understand your emotional problems and their healthy alternatives. Many years ago, a Stoic philosopher known as Epictetus wrote that people are disturbed not by adversities, but by the views that they take of these adversities. The REBT version of this is very similar. It is this:

> People are disturbed not by adversities, but by the rigid and extreme views that they take of these adversities.

I will go into this in greater depth later.

THE REBT VIEW OF HEALTHY ALTERNATIVES TO EMOTIONAL PROBLEMS

Unfortunately, Epictetus did not make clear how he would make sense of healthy alternatives to these emotional problems. Luckily REBT does. It is this:

> People can respond healthily to adversities by holding flexible and non-extreme views of these adversities.

Again, I will go into this in greater depth later.

REBT has what it calls the Situational ABC model of emotional problems and the healthy alternative to these problems that elaborates on the above. I will now present and discuss this model.

2

The Situational ABC Model

The Situational ABC model has four components: i) the situation; ii) the "A"; iii) the "B" and iv) the "C". I will discuss these one at a time.

SITUATION

You do not experience an emotional problem in a vacuum. Rather, there is almost always a situation in which you experience this problem. In considering this situation, bear in mind that it should reflect as accurately as possible the context in which you experienced your emotional problem.

"A"

When you experience an emotional problem in the situation that you are in, you usually disturb yourself about a particular aspect of this situation. In REBT, we call this the "A" or adversity.

"A" is Often an Inference

It is important to appreciate that your "A" is usually an inference that you have made about the situation or some aspect of the situation. An inference goes beyond the data at hand and can be accurate or inaccurate. Thus, if you receive a note from your boss that he wants to see you after lunch and you think: "He is going to criticise my work", then this thought is an inference since it goes beyond the facts of the situation. In this example, the facts are that your boss wants to see you after lunch. You do not know why. Your inference may be accurate or it may be inaccurate, but what makes it an inference is that it goes beyond the data at hand.

"A" Relates to your Personal Domain

An adversity (real or perceived) is usually related to some aspect of your "personal domain". The term "personal domain" was first introduced by Aaron Temkin Beck (1976), the founder of cognitive therapy (an approach to cognitive-behaviour therapy which shares certain ideas with REBT). It is made up of people, objects, concepts and ideas that are important to you. It also contains what is important to you about yourself. When you experience different unhealthy negative emotions, you disturb yourself about different adversities within your personal domain as shown below.

Adversity	Unhealthy Negative Emotion
Threat	Anxiety
Loss/failure	Depression
Breaking your moral code; failing to live up to your moral code; hurting someone	Guilt
Falling very short of your ideal in a social context	Shame
Someone betrays you or lets you down and you think you do not deserve such treatment	Hurt
Self or other transgresses a personal rule; other threatens self-esteem; frustration	Unhealthy anger
Threat to valued relationship	Unhealthy jealousy
Others have what you value and lack	Unhealthy envy

"B"

"B" stands for beliefs. In REBT beliefs can be irrational or rational.

Irrational Beliefs and Emotional Disturbance

As mentioned above, REBT's position on the major determinants of emotional problems can be summed up as follows: people are disturbed not by adversities, but by their rigid and extreme views of adversities. In REBT, these rigid and extreme views are known as irrational beliefs and as such are placed under "B" in the Situational ABC model. For example, looking at the above table, threats to your personal domain do not make you anxious. Rather you make yourself anxious by holding irrational beliefs about such threats.

Rational Beliefs and Emotional Health

Furthermore, REBT's position on emotional health can be summed up thus: people can respond healthily to adversities by holding flexible and non-extreme views of these adversities. In REBT, these flexible and non-extreme views are known as rational beliefs and they are also placed under "B" in the Situational ABC model. Thus, when we look again at the above table, you are concerned, but not anxious, about threats to your personal domain because you hold rational beliefs about such threats.

"C"

When you hold a set of beliefs about an adversity, REBT recognises that there are major consequences (at "C") of holding these beliefs.

Three Major Consequences of Beliefs

In REBT, we particularly look for three major consequences at "C" of beliefs at "B".

| ⊃ Emotional |
| ⊃ Behavioural and |
| ⊃ Thinking |

Consequences of Holding Irrational Beliefs

The influence of holding irrational beliefs on your emotions, behaviours and subsequent thinking can be summed up as follows:

When you face an adversity and your set of beliefs is irrational, the consequences of these beliefs are likely to be as follows:

C (emotional) = largely negative and unhealthy
C (behavioural) = largely dysfunctional
C (thinking) = largely negatively distorted and skewed

Consequences of Holding Rational Beliefs

The influence of holding rational beliefs on your emotions, behaviours and subsequent thinking can be summed up as follows:

When you face an adversity and your set of beliefs is rational the consequences of these beliefs are likely to be as follows:

C (emotional) = largely negative and healthy
C (behavioural) = largely functional
C (thinking) = largely realistic and balanced

3

Characteristics of Irrational
Beliefs and Rational Beliefs

As we have seen, the REBT model holds that irrational beliefs are at the core of emotional problems and rational beliefs are at the core of the solutions to these problems. Let me now discuss these beliefs since they are central to an understanding of how REBT makes sense of emotional problems and what constitutes healthy alternatives to these problems.

CHARACTERISTICS OF IRRATIONAL BELIEFS

Irrational beliefs are ideas that have the following characteristics. They are:

> ⊃ Rigid or extreme
> ⊃ Inconsistent with reality
> ⊃ Illogical or nonsensical
> ⊃ Largely unconstructive in their consequences

CHARACTERISTICS OF RATIONAL BELIEFS

On the other hand, rational beliefs are ideas that have the following characteristics. They are:

- ⊃ Flexible or non-extreme
- ⊃ Consistent with reality
- ⊃ Logical or sensible
- ⊃ Largely constructive in their consequences

REBT theory posits four irrational beliefs and their rational alternatives and I will introduce these one by one.

4

Demands Versus
Non-dogmatic Preferences

Albert Ellis, the founder of REBT, has argued that there are four main irrational beliefs that explain emotional problems in the face of life's adversities. These are: demands, awfulising beliefs, low frustration tolerance beliefs and depreciation beliefs. Of these, Ellis holds that demands lie at the very core of these problems. As such, for Ellis, they are the most important in accounting for unhealthy responses to life's adversities.

Ellis also said that there are four main rational beliefs that explain healthy responses to life's adversities. These are: non-dogmatic preferences, anti-awfulising beliefs, high frustration tolerance beliefs and acceptance beliefs. Of these, Ellis holds that non-dogmatic preferences lie at the very core of these healthy reactions. As such, for Ellis, they are the most important in accounting for healthy responses to life's adversities.

In this chapter, I will discuss demands and non-dogmatic preferences. I begin with demands.

DEMANDS

Demands are rigid ideas that you hold about how things absolutely must or must not be. Demands can be placed on:

> ⊃ Yourself (e.g. "I must be approved")
> ⊃ Others (e.g. "You must treat me fairly") or
> ⊃ Life conditions (e.g. "Life must be comfortable")

The healthy alternative to a demand is a non-dogmatic preference.

NON-DOGMATIC PREFERENCES

Non-dogmatic preferences are flexible ideas that you hold about how you would like things to be without demanding that they have to be that way. Non-dogmatic preferences can relate to:

> ⊃ Yourself (e.g. "I want to be approved, but I don't have to be")
> ⊃ Others (e.g. "I want you to treat me fairly, but regrettably you don't have to do so") or
> ⊃ Life conditions ("I very much want life to be comfortable, but unfortunately it doesn't have to be the way I want it to be")

TWO COMPONENTS OF NON-DOGMATIC PREFERENCES

If you look carefully at these beliefs you will see that they are made up of two components.

"Asserted Preference" Component

The first component puts forward what you want and is what I call the "asserted preference" component as shown in the following:

> ⊃ "I want to be approved . . ."
> ⊃ "I want you to treat me fairly . . ."
> ⊃ "I very much want life to be comfortable . . ."

"Negated Demand" Component

The second component acknowledges that you don't have to get what you want and is what I call the "negated demand" component, shown in italics below:

> ⊃ "I want to be approved, *but I don't have to be*"
> ⊃ "I want you to treat me fairly, *but regrettably you don't have to do so*"
> ⊃ "I very much want life to be comfortable, *but unfortunately it doesn't have to be the way I want it to be*"

5

Awfulising Beliefs Versus Anti-awfulising Beliefs

Awfulising beliefs and anti-awfulising beliefs are deemed in REBT theory to stem from demands and non-dogmatic preferences respectively.

AWFULISING BELIEFS

Awfulising beliefs are extreme ideas you hold about how bad it is when your demands are not met. Thus, as stated above, awfulising beliefs are derivatives from your demands when these demands aren't met. In the following examples the demands are listed in brackets.

> ⊃ "(I must be approved) . . . It is terrible if I am not approved"
> ⊃ "(You must treat me fairly) . . . It is awful when you treat me unfairly"
> ⊃ "(Life must be comfortable) . . . It is the end of the world when life is uncomfortable"

AWFULISING BELIEFS: WHAT YOU BELIEVE

An awfulising belief stems from the demand that things must not be as bad as they are and is extreme in the sense that you believe *at the time* one or more of the following:

1 Nothing could be worse
2 The event in question is worse than 100% bad and
3 No good could possibly come from this bad event

The healthy alternative to an awfulising belief is an anti-awfulising belief.

ANTI-AWFULISING BELIEFS

Anti-awfulising beliefs are non-extreme ideas you hold about how bad it is when your non-dogmatic preferences are not met. Thus, non-awfulising beliefs are derivatives from your non-dogmatic preferences when these non-dogmatic preferences aren't met. In the following examples the non-dogmatic preferences are in brackets.

⊃ "(I want to be approved, but I don't have to be.) It's bad if I am not approved, but not terrible"

⊃ "(I want you to treat me fairly, but regrettably you don't have to do so.) When you don't treat me fairly it's really bad, but not awful" and

⊃ "(I very much want life to be comfortable, but unfortunately it doesn't have to be that way.) If life is uncomfortable, that's very bad, but not the end of the world"

---

preparing you to give informed consent

TWO COMPONENTS OF ANTI-AWFULISING BELIEFS

If you look carefully at the anti-awfulising beliefs (i.e. the ones that are not in brackets) you will see that they are made up of two components.

"Asserted Badness" Component

The first component puts forward the idea that it is bad if you don't get what you want and is what I call the "asserted badness" component.

> ➲ "It's bad if I am not approved . . ."
> ➲ "When you don't treat me fairly, it's really bad . . ."
> ➲ "If life is uncomfortable, that's very bad . . ."

"Negated Awfulising" Component

The second component acknowledges that while it is bad if you don't get what you want, it is not terrible, awful or the end of the world. This is what I call the "negated awfulising" component. These are shown in italics below:

> ➲ "It's bad if I am not approved, *but not terrible*"
> ➲ "When you don't treat me fairly it's really bad, *but not awful*" and
> ➲ "If life is uncomfortable, that's very bad, *but not the end of the world*"

ANTI-AWFULISING BELIEFS: WHAT YOU BELIEVE

An anti-awfulising belief stems from the non-dogmatic preference that you would like things not to be as bad as they are, but that doesn't mean that they must not be as bad. This belief is non-extreme in the sense that you believe *at the time* one or more of the following:

1   Things could always be worse
2   The event in question is less than 100% bad and
3   Good could come from this bad event.

6

Low Frustration Tolerance Beliefs Versus High Frustration Tolerance Beliefs

Low frustration tolerance (LFT) beliefs and high frustration tolerance (HFT) beliefs are deemed in REBT theory to stem from demands and non-dogmatic preferences respectively.

LFT BELIEFS

LFT beliefs are extreme ideas that you hold about the tolerability of events when your demands are not met. Thus LFT beliefs are derivatives from your demands when these demands aren't met. In the following examples the demands are listed in brackets.

- ⊃ "(I must be approved.) I can't bear it if I am not approved"
- ⊃ "(You must treat me fairly.) It is intolerable when you don't treat me fairly" and
- ⊃ "(Life must be comfortable.) I can't stand it when it is uncomfortable"

LFT BELIEFS: WHAT YOU BELIEVE

An LFT belief stems from the demand that things must not be as frustrating or uncomfortable as they are and is extreme in the sense that you believe *at the time* one or more of the following:

1   I will die or disintegrate if the frustration or discomfort continues to exist
2   I will lose the capacity to experience happiness if the frustration or discomfort continues to exist

The healthy alternative to a low frustration tolerance belief is an HFT belief.

HFT BELIEFS

HFT beliefs are non-extreme ideas that you hold about the tolerability of events when your non-dogmatic preferences are not met. Thus HFT beliefs are derivatives from your non-dogmatic preferences when these are not met. In the following examples the non-dogmatic preferences are in brackets.

- ⊃   "(I want to be approved, but I don't have to be.) When I am not approved it is difficult to bear, but I can bear it and it's worth bearing because I don't want to live my life worried about disapproval"
- ⊃   "(I want you to treat me fairly, but regrettably you don't have to do so.) When you don't treat me fairly it's really hard to tolerate, but I can tolerate it and it's worth it to me to do so because I don't want to be overly affected about what you do" and

---

preparing you to give informed consent

> ⊃ "(I very much want life to be comfortable, but unfortunately it doesn't have to be the way I want it to be.) If life is uncomfortable, that's hard to stand, but I can stand it and it is in my best interests to do so because I want to get on with life"

THREE COMPONENTS OF HFT BELIEFS

If you look carefully at the high frustration tolerance beliefs (i.e. the ones that are not in brackets) you will see that they are made up of three components.

"Asserted Struggle" Component

The first component puts forward the idea that it is difficult tolerating not getting what you want and is what I call the "asserted struggle" component.

> ⊃ "When I am not approved, it is difficult to bear . . ."
> ⊃ "When you don't treat me fairly, it's really hard to tolerate . . ."
> ⊃ "If life is uncomfortable, that's hard to stand . . ."

"Negated Unbearability" Component

The second component acknowledges that while it is a struggle to put up with what you don't want, it is possible to do so and that it isn't unbearable. This is what I call the "negated unbearability" component. This component is shown in italics in the examples below:

> ↺ "When I am not approved it is difficult to bear, *but I can bear it . . ."*
>
> ↺ "When you don't treat me fairly it's really hard to tolerate, *but I can tolerate it . . ."* and
>
> ↺ "If life is uncomfortable, that's hard to stand, *but I can stand it . . ."*

"Worth Bearing" Component

The third component addresses the point that it is often worth it to you to tolerate the situation where you don't get what you want. This is what I call the "worth bearing" component. This component is shown in italics in the examples below. Note that in each case the reason why it is worth tolerating is specified.

> ↺ "When I am not approved it is difficult to bear, but I can bear it *and it's worth bearing because I don't want to live my life worried about disapproval"*
>
> ↺ "When you don't treat me fairly it's really hard to tolerate, but I can tolerate it *and it's worth it to me to do so because I don't want to be overly affected about what you do"* and
>
> ↺ "If life is uncomfortable, that's hard to stand, but I can stand it *and it is in my best interests to do so because I want to get on with life"*

HFT BELIEFS: WHAT YOU BELIEVE

An HFT belief stems from the non-dogmatic preference that it is undesirable when things are as frustrating or uncomfortable as they are, but unfortunately things don't have to be different. It is non-extreme in the sense that you believe *at the time* one or more of the following:

1   I will struggle if the frustration or discomfort continues to exist, but I will neither die nor disintegrate
2   I will not lose the capacity to experience happiness if the frustration or discomfort continues to exist, although this capacity will be temporarily diminished and
3   The frustration or discomfort is worth tolerating.

7

Depreciation Beliefs
Versus Acceptance Beliefs

Depreciation beliefs and acceptance beliefs are deemed in REBT theory to stem from demands and non-dogmatic preferences respectively.

DEPRECIATION BELIEFS

Depreciation beliefs are extreme ideas that you hold about self, other(s) and/or the world when you don't get what you demand. As such, and as stated above, depreciation beliefs are derivatives from your demands when these demands aren't met. In the following examples the demands are listed in brackets.

⊃ "(I must be approved.) I am worthless if am not approved"
⊃ "(You must treat me fairly.) You are a bad person if you don't treat me fairly
⊃ "(Life must be comfortable.) The world is bad if life isn't comfortable"

DEPRECIATION BELIEFS: WHAT YOU BELIEVE

A depreciation belief stems from the demand that you, others or things must be as you want them to be and is extreme in the sense that you believe *at the time* one or more of the following:

1 A person (self or other) can legitimately be given a single global rating that defines their essence and the worth of a person is dependent upon conditions that change (e.g. my worth goes up when I do well and goes down when I don't do well)
2 The world can legitimately be given a single rating that defines its essential nature and the value of the world varies according to what happens within it (e.g. the value of the world goes up when something fair occurs and goes down when something unfair happens)
3 A person can be rated on the basis of one of his or her aspects and the world can be rated on the basis of one of its aspects

The healthy alternative to a depreciation belief is an acceptance belief.

ACCEPTANCE BELIEFS

Acceptance beliefs are non-extreme ideas that you hold about self, other(s) and/or the world when you don't get what you want, but do not demand that you have to get what you want. As such, acceptance beliefs are derivatives from your non-dogmatic preferences when these non-dogmatic preferences aren't met. In the following examples the non-dogmatic preferences are in brackets.

- ⊃ "(I want to be approved, but I don't have to be.) When I am not approved that is bad, but I am not worthless. I am a fallible human being who is not being approved on this occasion"
- ⊃ "(I want you to treat me fairly, but regrettably you don't have to do so.) When you don't treat me fairly that is very unfortunate, but you are not a bad person. Rather, you are a fallible human being who is treating me unfairly" and
- ⊃ "(I very much want life to be comfortable, but unfortunately it doesn't have to be the way I want it to be.) If life is uncomfortable it is only uncomfortable in this respect and doesn't prove that the world is a rotten place. The world is a complex place where many good, bad and neutral things happen"

THREE COMPONENTS OF ACCEPTANCE BELIEFS

If you look carefully at the acceptance beliefs (i.e. the ones that are not in brackets) you will see that they are made up of three components.

"Evaluation of a Part of Self or what has Happened to Self" Component

The first component acknowledges that it is possible and realistic to evaluate a part of oneself or what has happened to oneself as shown in italics below:

- ⊃ "When I am not approved *that is bad* . . ."
- ⊃ "When you don't treat me fairly *that is very regrettable* . . ."
- ⊃ "If life is uncomfortable *it is only uncomfortable in this respect* . . ."

"Negation of Depreciation" Component

The second component puts forward the idea that it is not possible to evaluate globally a person or life conditions when you don't get what you want. I call this the "negation of depreciation" component. These are shown in italics below:

> ○ When I am not approved that is bad, *but I am not worthless . . ."*
>
> ○ "When you don't treat me fairly that is very regrettable, *but you are not a bad person . . ."*
>
> ○ "If life is uncomfortable it is only uncomfortable in this respect *and doesn't prove that the world is a rotten place . . ."*

"Assertion of Acceptance" Component

The third component asserts the idea that when you don't get what you want, this does not affect the fallibility of people and the complexity of life. This is what I call the "assertion of acceptance" component. These are shown in italics below:

> ○ "When I am not approved that is bad, but I am not worthless. *I am a fallible human being who is not being approved on this occasion"*
>
> ○ "When you don't treat me fairly that is very regrettable, but you are not a bad person. *Rather you are a fallible human being who is treating me unfairly"*
>
> ○ "If life is uncomfortable it is only uncomfortable in this respect and doesn't prove that the world is a rotten place. *The world is a complex place where many good, bad and neutral things happen"*

ACCEPTANCE BELIEFS: WHAT YOU BELIEVE

An acceptance belief is non-extreme in the sense that you believe *at the time* one or more of the following:

1   A person cannot legitimately be given a single global rating that defines their essence and their worth, as far as they have it, is not dependent upon conditions that change (e.g. my worth stays the same whether or not I do well)
2   The world cannot legitimately be given a single rating that defines its essential nature and the value of the world does not vary according to what happens within it (e.g. the value of the world stays the same whether fairness exists at any given time or not)
3   It makes sense to rate discrete aspects of a person and of the world, but it does not make sense to rate a person or the world on the basis of these discrete aspects

You now have an understanding of how REBT conceptualises emotional problems and healthy alternatives to these problems. Let me now turn my attention to the practice of REBT.

II

The Practice of Rational Emotive Behaviour Therapy

The practice of REBT has a number of features and it is important that you understand what these are before you commit yourself to using REBT either as a self-help therapy or with an REBT therapist.

8

REBT is Problem-focused

In REBT we encourage you to focus directly on your emotional problems. You will be invited to deal with your problems one at a time, at least at the outset and you will be helped to assess them using REBT's Situational ABC model which I briefly discussed in Chapter 2 and which I will discuss in Section IV in Part 2 of the book. You will then be equipped to deal with the factors responsible for maintaining these problems.

9

REBT is Goal-directed

As you work on your emotional problems you will be encouraged to set realistic goals for each of these problems. These are based on helping you to respond to adversities with healthy negative feelings, functional behaviour and realistic subsequent thinking as a prelude to changing these adversities if they can be changed and to adjusting constructively to them if they cannot.

10

REBT is Structured and Logical in its Practice

Once you have nominated a problem on which to work (known as the "target problem" in REBT circles), the way you are helped to deal with this problem is both structured and logical. With respect to structure, REBT has a situationally-based ABC model (which I introduced to you in Chapter 2 and which will be discussed more fully in Chapters 19-23), a structure which helps you to assess specific examples of your target problem and to identify their important components. Thus, you will be helped to:

> ⊃ Describe as objectively as possible the situation in which your emotional problem occurs
>
> ⊃ Identify your disturbed emotive, behavioural and thinking reactions at "C"
>
> ⊃ Specify what you were disturbed about in the situation at hand (known as the adversity at "A")
>
> ⊃ Identify your irrational beliefs at "B" about "A" that largely determined "C"
>
> ⊃ Set goals for healthier responses at "C" to the adversity at "A" and then see what your rational beliefs could be which would underpin these healthier responses

preparing you to give informed consent

- ⊃ Question your beliefs so that you commit yourself to strengthening your conviction in your rational beliefs and weakening your conviction in your irrational beliefs
- ⊃ Use methods of achieving such conviction change that will enable you to deal constructively with your targeted emotional problem

11

REBT has an Educational Focus

In REBT, we believe that we can *teach* people to overcome their emotional problems. As I noted earlier, REBT has a specific point of view in explaining disturbance. We believe in being open and explicit about REBT's viewpoint on emotional problems and this is one way in which REBT is educationally focused. The other way is that you will be shown how to apply REBT methods of bringing about psychological change. This is what I will endeavour to demonstrate to you in Part 2. If you are consulting an REBT therapist, he or she will teach you these methods in ways that are tailored to your unique situation (something that I unfortunately cannot do in this book).

12

REBT is Primarily Present-centred and Future-oriented

While REBT will help you with whatever emotional problems you have, you will be encouraged to consider problems that you are facing in the here and now and those that you anticipate in the future. Having said this, REBT does not neglect your past and will help you deal with it in two major ways. First, REBT will help you to identify and deal with your present feelings about past events. Second, it will help you to see that when you were disturbed in the past, this was largely because of the irrational beliefs that you held at that time and which you have unwittingly maintained in the present. It will then help you to question and change these beliefs so that you can have healthy negative feelings now about past adversities.

13

REBT has a Skills Emphasis

As I showed in the extended companion to this book entitled *Reason to Change: A Rational Emotive Behaviour Therapy (REBT) Workbook* (Dryden 2001), REBT specifies a number of skills that you can learn and use once formal therapy is over. In that book, I detailed those skills and showed what people needed to do in order to learn them. This skills emphasis is a feature of REBT in general and the present book in particular.

14

In REBT, the Therapist is Largely Active and Directive

If you are thinking of consulting an REBT therapist and using this book as an adjunct to that work, it may be helpful for you to know at the outset that your therapist will, in all probability, adopt an active-directive style, particularly at the beginning of therapy. As I mentioned above, REBT is a problem-oriented and problem-solving approach to counselling and psychotherapy and as such your REBT therapist will be active and directive in the following ways. He or she will help you to:

⊃ Identify and formulate your emotional problems
⊃ Set goals with respect to these problems
⊃ Work with one problem at a time
⊃ Assess specific instances of these problems
⊃ Question your beliefs (both irrational and rational) and
⊃ Help you to strengthen your conviction in your rational beliefs.

If your therapist took an inactive, non-directive therapeutic style, he or she would fail to help you to use REBT effectively. If you want to explore your problems in an open, unstructured way, REBT is not for you, but if you want your therapist to direct you in an active manner to factors that are responsible for the origin and maintenance of your emotional problems so that you can deal with these factors in an efficient manner, then REBT is for you, assuming that you think you can use its main ideas which I previously outlined.

15

The Process of REBT

In Chapter 10, entitled "REBT is Structured and Logical in its Practice", I briefly outlined how REBT tackles a given emotional problem. However, most people have more than one emotional problem and if this is the case with you, you may find it helpful to understand a little of the process of REBT from beginning to end.

1   Initially, you will use REBT with an example of your target problem.
2   Then, you will be encouraged to transfer the skills that you have learned from doing so to other examples of your target problem.
3   After doing so, you will be helped to generalise your learning further to specific examples of your other target problems. This is where this book is particularly useful in that it aims to show you:

   a) The inferential themes that occur at "A" in the ABC framework for each of the eight major emotional problems for which people seek therapeutic help - i.e. anxiety, depression, guilt, shame, hurt, unhealthy anger, unhealthy jealousy and unhealthy envy (see Chapter 2) and

b) The behavioural and thinking consequences of irrational beliefs about "A" and those that stem from rational beliefs about the same "A".

4   As you progress, you will be helped to identify one or more core irrational beliefs that underpin your different emotional problems and will be encouraged to identify an alternative set of core rational beliefs. During this process you will be helped to identify particular ways in which you avoid dealing constructively with your emotional problems, how you unwittingly perpetuate your core irrational beliefs and how you over-compensate for them. You will be encouraged to face up to your problems, deal with the maintaining factors and desist from using over-compensatory strategies.

5   Since the process of REBT, like the path of true love, rarely runs smoothly, a main feature of the process of REBT involves helping you to identify and deal effectively with any obstacles to change.

6   Towards the end of the process you will also be encouraged to maintain your gains by helping yourself to prevent relapse. This basically involves you identifying and dealing effectively with vulnerability factors and learning from small lapses in progress.

7   While you will be encouraged to take responsibility for your therapy at the outset, towards the very end of the REBT process you will be encouraged to function as your own therapist and at this point your REBT therapist is likely to operate as a consultant rather than as a therapist, helping you to fine-tune your REBT skills and identifying subtle obstacles to change that you may have overlooked.

Please note that this book covers only the first four of the above seven steps.

16

It's Decision Time

I said at the beginning of Part 1 that by its end you should have sufficient information about REBT to make an informed judgement concerning its utility in helping you deal with your emotional problems. You should now be in a position to be able to do this. So, if you wish to give your informed consent to proceed, I look forward to helping you. You should now turn to Part 2 where I outline common issues that arise in REBT no matter which emotional problem or problems you are seeking help for. However, if you think that REBT is not for you, thank you for your consideration. You might find a consumer's guide to different approaches to counselling and psychotherapy that I wrote with a colleague of use in finding an approach that is better suited to you (Dryden and Feltham 1995).

PART 2

Dealing with Emotional Problems Using Rational Emotive Behaviour Therapy

As you are now reading the second part of this book, I am going to assume that you have read the first part and have decided that you wish to proceed and use REBT to address your emotional problems either on your own or with an REBT therapist I am making the assumption, therefore, that you have given your informed consent to proceed.

In this part of the book, I am going to deal with a number of issues that are relevant no matter what your emotional problems are. In the main I will help you to do four things. These are:

1 Formulate your emotional problems and set goals with respect to these problems
2 Assess specific examples of your emotional problems using the "Situational ABC" framework and set goals with respect to dealing with these specific examples
3 Question your irrational and rational beliefs
4 Strengthen your conviction in your rational beliefs

In addition, I will help you to:

- ⊃ Identify and deal with any meta-emotional problems that you may have
- ⊃ Identify and correct your distorted inferences and
- ⊃ Identify and question your core irrational beliefs and develop conviction in your core rational beliefs

III

Formulate Problems
and Set Goals

The first step in helping yourself with REBT is to be clear with yourself what your problems are and what your goals are with respect to these problems.

17

Formulate Your Emotional Problems

I suggest that you use the following steps in formulating each of your emotional problems:

1   **[Situations]** - Identify the situations in which you experience your problem.
2   **[A]** - Identify the theme of the problem. Ask yourself what is it about the situations that you specified that is a problem for you. This is likely to be an inference. Consult the table in Chapter 2 for help on this point (see p. 10).
3   **[C (Emotional)]** - Identify the *one* major unhealthy negative emotion that you experience when you encounter the situations and theme that you specified above.
4   **[C (Behavioural)]** - Identify the dysfunctional behaviour that you demonstrate in these situations.
5   **[C (Thinking)]** - Identify the thinking you engage in once your unhealthy negative emotion has "kicked in".

Here is an example.

1	Type of situation: *When any of my friends go out without me* **[Situations]**
2	Theme: *I think that they don't want to be with me* **[A]**
3	Major unhealthy negative emotion: *Hurt* **[C (Emotional)]**
4	Behaviour: *I withdraw from them* **[C (Behavioural)]**
5	Thinking: *Everyone will think that I am boring* **[C Thinking)]**

Putting this into a sentence we have: "When any of my friends go out without me, I think that they don't want to be with me. I feel hurt about this and withdraw from them and think that everyone will think that I'm boring."

18

Set Goals

Every human being has goals that they aim towards, things that they would like to do or to have. However, a lot of the time most people are unclear about what their goals are at any given period in their lives. Their goals are often implicit and unstated, even to themselves. An *adversity* is a situation that conflicts with, or gets in the way of, our goals. An important part of therapy is specifying your goals and in this chapter I will help you set goals for each of your emotional problems.

I suggest that you use the following steps in setting goals for each of your emotional problems:

1 **[Situations]** - Identify the situations in which you experience your problem. This will be the same as you listed in the "situations" section of your formulated problem in Chapter 17.

2 **[A]** - Identify the theme of the problem. Ask yourself what is it about the situations that you specified that is a problem for you. This is likely to be an inference and will be the same as you listed under "A" in your formulated problem.

3 **[C (Emotional goal)]** - Identify the healthy alternative to the major unhealthy negative emotion that you experience when you encounter the situations and theme that you specified above. Note that this emotional goal should

dealing with emotional problems

be negative because it is about an adversity, but it should also be healthy in the sense that it will enable you to deal effectively with the adversity if it can be changed or you can adjust constructively to it if it cannot be changed.

4   **[C (Behavioural goal)]** - Identify the functional alternative to the unconstructive behaviour that you demonstrated.

5   **[C (Thinking goal)]** - Identify the realistic alternative to the distorted thinking that you engaged in.

Note that when you set goals for your emotional problems, you are only changing your emotional, behavioural and thinking responses to the situations and to the themes in these situations that you find problematic. This is because in REBT we want you to be prepared to face life's adversities even when you think that an adversity will happen when in fact it doesn't.

Here are the goals set by the person whose emotional problem was formulated above in Chapter 17. As noted, the first two steps are the same in the goal section as in the formulated problem section.

---

1   Type of situation: *When any of my friends go out without me*
    [Situations]

2   Theme: *I think that they don't want to be with me*
    [A]

3   Major unhealthy negative emotion: *Sorrow (rather than hurt)*
    [C (Emotional goal)]

4   Behaviour: *To communicate my sorrow to them (rather than withdraw from them)*
    [C (Behavioural goal)]

---

5 Thinking: *To think that people will have a range of responses to me (rather than think that everyone will think that I am boring)*
   [C (Thinking goal)]

Putting this into a sentence we have: "When any of my friends go out without me and I think that they don't want to be with me, I want to feel sorrow rather than hurt about this and to communicate how I feel rather than withdraw from them. I also want to think that people will have a range of responses to me rather than think that everyone will think that I'm boring."

Note that under the headings of "emotional goal", "behavioural goal" and "thinking goal", I suggest that you use the "rather than" wording to highlight the difference between your problem response and your goal response. However, if you find doing this cumbersome, then omit the "rather than" phrases.

IV

Assess Specific Examples
of Your Emotional Problems

Once you have formulated your emotional problems and set goals for each of them it is important that you work on one problem at a time. If you attempt to work on more than one problem at a time or if you switch between problems you will derive less benefit from REBT than if you focus on one problem and work though this problem. When you focus on and work on one of your formulated problems, this problem is known as your *target problem*.

The best way to work on target problems is to choose a *specific example* of this problem. Such an example might be a recent situation in which your target problem occurred or it may be one that stands out in your mind. The main reason for working with a specific example of a target problem is that since you disturb yourself in specific situations, analysis of such situations provides you and your REBT therapist (if you are working with one) with the necessary information needed to understand precisely how you disturbed yourself and thus what you need to focus on so that you learn to undisturb yourself in such contexts. The first step in this process is an accurate assessment of your selected specific example of your target problem. What follows, then, is a series of steps to enable you to get the most from this assessment process.

19

Describe the "Situation"

Once you have selected a specific example of your target problem, the first thing to do is to describe the situation in which you felt disturbed. As you do so, it is important that your description be as objective as possible. Imagine that you are a video camera with an audio channel. This is the level of objectivity you are aiming for. Try to keep all subjective elements out of your description. You will have an opportunity to include these, if relevant, when you are assessing the "A".

Here are some examples of objective descriptions of "situations":

> ↄ *Freddie told me that he wanted to change the time of our appointment*
> ↄ *My mother invited me to dinner last night*
> ↄ *When I thought about going to the dentist, my hands began to shake*

20

Identify Your Disturbed Reactions at "C"

After you have described the situation you are in, the next stage is to identify your disturbed reactions to this situation at "C" in the ABC framework. This involves identifying your major unhealthy negative emotion (UNE), the dysfunctional way you acted or felt like acting and your distorted subsequent thoughts. Let me consider these one at a time.

IDENTIFY YOUR MAJOR UNE

After you have described the situation in which you disturbed yourself you need to identify the *major* UNE that you felt in that situation. Doing so at this point will enable you to identify what you were most disturbed about at "A" (see Chapter 21). Here are some tips to help you to identify your major UNE.

LOOK AT YOUR FORMULATED PROBLEM FOR YOUR SPECIFIC UNE

In Chapter 17, I showed you how to formulate your problems. In that formulation your UNE played a prominent role, so when you experience one of your formulated problems in a specific situation, it should be easy to identify your specific UNE, since it will be substantially the same emotion as the one listed in your formulated problem. For example, let's suppose that your formulated problem is: "When any of my friends go out without me, I think that they don't want to be with me. *I feel hurt* about this and withdraw from them and think that everyone will think that I'm boring." Then, if the situation in your specific example was "My friend Sally went out without me", then your specific UNE is likely to be "hurt".

COMMON UNEs

However, there are times when you may disturb yourself about other matters that are not covered by your formulated problems. As such you have to start from scratch in identifying the main unhealthy negative emotion that you experienced in this situation. It is important that you are specific in identifying your UNE since being so will help you to identify the other elements in the ABC framework. If you have some difficulty in working out how you are feeling, you may find the following list useful as the emotions listed represent the main UNEs for which people seek help:

⊃ Anxiety
⊃ Depression
⊃ Guilt
⊃ Shame
⊃ Hurt
⊃ Unhealthy anger
⊃ Unhealthy jealousy
⊃ Unhealthy envy

WHAT IF YOU HAVE MORE THAN ONE UNE IN THE SITUATION?

You can have more than one feeling in any given situation. Thus, imagine that your boss has just criticised a piece of work in front of your colleagues and you feel hurt and ashamed. You may feel hurt about being unfairly criticised by a boss who you previously thought was supportive of you:

A = *My boss unfairly criticised me*
iB = *Not yet known*
C = *Hurt*

And you may feel ashamed about appearing foolish in front of others:

A = *I am appearing foolish in front of others*
iB = *Not yet known*
C = *Ashamed*

In such situations, choose the UNE that represents your biggest problem and work with that one first. However, at this point, what is more important is that once you have chosen one UNE you stick with this problem until you have dealt with it before switching to the other problem.

THE DIFFERENCE BETWEEN HEALTHY AND UNHEALTHY NEGATIVE EMOTIONS

Another problem that often occurs in identifying the emotional C involves differentiating healthy negative emotions (HNEs) from UNEs. Sometimes people misunderstand the difference between these two and try to change an HNE. For example, Susan is training to be a vet and has important exams to take. She is keen to do well, but has unpleasant and uncomfortable butterfly feelings in her stomach when she thinks about the exams that do not interfere with her revision. In this case her feelings of concern represent an HNE and this emotion is determined by a rational belief. Anxiety, however, is a UNE and is created by an irrational belief. Were Susan to try and change her feelings of concern, she would be trying to change a healthy emotion, albeit negative.

The three major ways of distinguishing between HNEs and UNEs are a) beliefs (irrational in UNEs; rational in HNEs); b) associated behaviour (dysfunctional in UNEs, functional in HNEs); and c) associated thinking (highly unrealistic in UNEs, realistic in HNEs).

IDENTIFY YOUR DYSFUNCTIONAL BEHAVIOUR

As I pointed out above, when you experience a UNE your associated behaviour is likely to be dysfunctional and as such it will exacerbate your emotional problem. There are two types of behaviour that you need to identify at "C": actual behaviours that are observable and action tendencies where you "feel like" acting in a certain way, but do not. There are certain forms of behaviour that are frequently associated with particular UNEs. I provide a representative list below.

UNE	Dysfunctional Behaviours and Action Tendencies
Anxiety	Withdrawing from threat; avoiding threat; seeking reassurance even though not reassurable; seeking safety from threat
Depression	Prolonged withdrawal from enjoyable activities
Guilt	Begging for forgiveness
Shame	Withdrawing from others; avoiding eye contact with others
Hurt	Sulking
Unhealthy anger	Aggression (direct and indirect)
Unhealthy jealousy	Prolonged suspicious questioning of the other person; checking on the other; restricting the other
Unhealthy envy	Spoiling the other's enjoyment of the desired possession

IDENTIFY YOUR SUBSEQUENT DISTORTED THINKING

When you feel a UNE and act in a dysfunctional way at "C", you also tend to think in ways that are highly distorted and exaggerated. I call this thinking "subsequent distorted thinking" because it stems from irrational beliefs and because it is distorted in nature. There are certain forms of thinking that are frequently associated with particular UNEs. I provide a representative list below.

UNE	Subsequent Distorted Thinking
Anxiety	Overestimating the negative consequences of the threat if it occurs
Depression	Hopelessness; helplessness
Guilt	Assigning too much responsibility to self and too little to others
Shame	Overestimating the negativity of others' reactions to self and the extent of these reactions
Hurt	Thinking that the other has to put things right of their own accord
Unhealthy anger	Thinking that the other has malicious intent; thoughts of exacting revenge
Unhealthy jealousy	Tending to see threats to one's relationship in the absence of evidence
Unhealthy envy	Tending to denigrate the value of the desired possession

21

Identify Your "A"

The next stage is to identify your "A". Remember that "A" is an adversity. It is the subjective aspect of the situation that you were in that you were most disturbed about. If the episode you are analysing is a specific example of your target problem, then the "A" in this example will reflect the theme in your problem. For example, let's take the formulated problem outlined in Chapter 17: "When any of my friends go out without me, I think that they don't want to be with me. I feel hurt about this and withdraw from them and think that everyone will think that I'm boring." If this person selected a specific example of this target problem, then one would expect the "A" to be "One of my friends did not want to be with me." If this is not the case for you, then you would do the following:

1   Focus on the "situation" that you have described
2   Ask yourself what one thing would get rid of or significantly diminish the unhealthy negative emotion that you felt at "C"
3   The opposite to this is your "A"

Here is an example of using these three points in identifying the "A". The described situation is: "My father said that he was going to give me a house-warming present." The person's "C" was anxiety:

1   Focus on the "situation" that you have described = *My father said that he was going to give me a house-warming present*
2   Ask yourself what one thing would get rid of or significantly diminish the anxiety that you felt at "C" = *My father not using this against me at a later date*
3   The opposite to this is your "A" = *My father using this present against me at a later date*

Identifying "A" is particularly important in that it is "A" which triggers the irrational belief ("iB") which leads to the disturbed emotional, behavioural and thinking reactions at "C". As such, do not at this point challenge "A" even if it is obviously distorted. Assume temporarily that it is true. This is so important, let me emphasise it.

Once you have identified "A", assume temporarily that it is true. Do not challenge it at this point even if it is obviously distorted.

22

Identify Your
Goals in the ABC

In Chapter 18, I showed you how to set goals for your formulated emotional and behavioural problems. It is also important to set goals when you are working on a specific example of your target problem or when you are analysing any specific episode of self-disturbance.

When you encounter a specific adversity at "A", you can either think rationally or irrationally about the fact that your goals are blocked. If you think rationally about this adversity, you will experience a healthy negative emotion which will assist you to behave in a way that is likely to help you get back on track in pursuing your goal if this can be reached, or find some other valued goal to replace it if your original goal can't be reached. Also, your subsequent thinking will be realistic and help you to focus on what you need to do to change the situation or constructively adjust to it if it cannot be changed. However, if you think irrationally about the adversity, you will feel an unhealthy negative emotion and, as we have seen, will behave and think in ways that worsen the problem rather than improve it.

In its practical use, the ABC model starts with a "situation" which, as we have noted, is an objective description of the context you were in when you disturbed yourself at "C" about an adversity at "A". The presence of "A" is a sign that one of your goals has been blocked and "C" stands for your reactions to this adversity which are largely the emotional, behavioural and thinking consequences of the beliefs that you held about "A".

A major purpose of the ABC framework when you have a disturbed reaction at "C" is to work out the irrational beliefs at "B" that largely determine these disturbed reactions, and I will cover this subject in depth presently. But before this it is very useful to see how you would have liked to have responded at "C" to the specific adversity at "A" instead of your disturbed reaction

Let me demonstrate the process of goal-setting using a specific example of an ABC.

GINA

Gina was told by her friend that she saw Gina's boyfriend eating out with another woman. This is the "situation". Gina thinks that this means that her boyfriend probably wants to end their relationship ("A") and responds with anxiety (emotional "C"), constantly phoning her boyfriend for reassurance that he loves her (behavioural "C") and thinking of her boyfriend making love with this other woman. So far we have:

"Situation" = *My friend told me that she saw my boyfriend eating with another woman*

"A" = *He will probably want to end our relationship*

"iB" (Irrational belief) = *Not yet known*

"C" (Emotional) = *Anxiety*

(Behavioural) = *Constantly phoning boyfriend for reassurance that he still loves me*

(Thinking) = *Thinking of boyfriend making love with the other woman*

Remember, neither the "situation" (Gina's friend telling her that she saw Gina's boyfriend eating with another woman) nor the "A" (Gina's inference that her boyfriend will probably want to end their relationship) caused the consequences of her feeling anxious, constantly ringing her boyfriend for reassurance and thinking of her boyfriend making love to the other woman. Gina *created these consequences herself* largely by her own irrational beliefs. The point of Gina using the ABC model is to work out what her irrational beliefs are and then change them to rational beliefs. This is "B" in the ABC framework.

Before Gina does this, she needs to establish a goal: what she wants to achieve in the situation under consideration. This is an important consideration since unless Gina knows what she wants to achieve, she won't be very focused on what to tackle.

Gina's friend telling her about seeing her boyfriend eating out with another woman is a potentially bad situation for Gina. Her thought that he will probably want to end their relationship is a particular adversity for her since if this were true, it would go against her goal to have a continued relationship with her boyfriend. Obviously, if he were to end the relationship this would block that goal. Therefore, Gina's "A" is an adversity. Now, Gina may not be able to change the situation because her boyfriend is in charge of his decision to end or maintain their relationship. However, Gina can change her emotional, behavioural and thinking consequences. The question is, change them to what?

Gina's Emotional Goal

Let's start with Gina's feelings. Would it be healthy for Gina to feel happy, or even calm, about her boyfriend wanting to end their relationship? Hardly! To achieve this, Gina would have to fool herself into believing either it was good that there was a possibility of being dumped (as she put it) or that she didn't care that such a possibility existed. It is very unlikely that either of these approaches will help Gina, and they certainly won't make the problem go away. A healthier, but realistic, emotional alternative to anxiety about her boyfriend wanting to end their relationship would be for Gina to feel *concerned* about this prospect, but not anxious about it.

Gina's Behavioural Goal

What about her behavioural goal? Asking her boyfriend about the identity of the "mystery" woman and the nature of their relationship is a reasonable behavioural goal since it is important for Gina to discover whether or not there is a threat to her relationship with her boyfriend. In this way she can assess his answer and estimate the actual threat to her relationship. Constantly phoning him to seek reassurance that he still loves her does not help her to estimate this threat.

Gina's Subsequent Thinking Goal

Finally, what about her subsequent thinking goal? Clearly imagining her boyfriend making love to the woman he was seen eating out with is unhealthy. Instead of dong this, Gina chose to work towards thinking about how she would raise the issue of the identity of the other woman and the nature of their relationship.

Here is Gina's ABC updated with her goals:

dealing with emotional problems

"Situation" = *My friend told me that she saw my boyfriend eating with another woman* "A" = *He will probably want to end our relationship*	
"iB" (Irrational belief) = *Not yet known* "C" (Emotional) = *Anxiety* (Behavioural) = *Constantly phoning boyfriend for reassurance that he still loves me* (Thinking) = *Thinking of boyfriend making love with the other woman*	"rB" (Rational belief) = *Not yet known* "C" (Emotional goal) = *Concern* (Behavioural goal) = *Ask boyfriend about the identity of the woman he ate out with and the nature of their relationship, and assess his answer logically* (Thinking goal) = *Consider the best way of raising the issue with boyfriend*

The next step is to work out what set of irrational beliefs ("iBs") Gina has about the possibility of her boyfriend ending their relationship and what are the rational alternatives to these beliefs. But before I do this, I want to outline a) the healthy alternatives to the eight unhealthy negative emotions that I listed in Chapter 20; b) the common functional behaviours/action tendencies that are associated with these HNEs and c) the type of realistic thinking that is associated with each of these HNEs. You should consult Chapter 20 if you need help in formulating your goals in dealing with specific episodes of self-disturbance.

REBT theory states that when you are facing an adversity at "A" then it is healthy for you to have negative feelings about that adversity. Such feelings are realistic responses to adversities and help you to change these adversities if they can be changed.

However, you may struggle to think of what constitutes a healthy negative feeling response to an adversity. Unfortunately, we do not have good words in the English language to describe HNEs. The following list reflects my own usage which you may find helpful. If not, use your own language.

Unhealthy Negative Emotions	Healthy Negative Emotions
Anxiety	Concern
Depression	Sadness
Guilt	Remorse
Shame	Disappointment
Hurt	Sorrow
Unhealthy anger	Healthy anger
Unhealthy jealousy	Healthy jealousy
Unhealthy envy	Healthy envy

You can use this list to help you to specify your emotional goals in dealing with specific episodes of self-disturbance and in setting broad goals for change (see Chapter 18).

Functional Behaviours and Action Tendencies Associated with Healthy Negative Emotions

As I pointed out above, when you experience an HNE, your associated behaviour is likely to be functional. There are two types of behaviour that you need to identify as goals in the ABC framework: actual behaviours that are observable and action tendencies (i.e. urges to act). There are certain forms of behaviour that are frequently associated with particular HNEs. I provide a representative list below. This should be compared with the list of dysfunctional behaviours associated with UNEs that I presented in Chapter 20.

You should consult the list below if you need help in identifying functional behavioural goals.

Healthy Negative Emotion	Functional Behaviours and Action Tendencies
Concern (as opposed to anxiety)	Confronting threat; seeking reassurance when reassurable
Sadness (as opposed to depression)	Engaging with enjoyable activities after a period of mourning or adjustment to the loss
Remorse (as opposed to guilt)	Asking, not begging, for forgiveness
Disappointment (as opposed to shame)	Keeping in contact with others, maintaining eye contact with others
Sorrow (as opposed to hurt)	Assertion and communicating with others

Healthy anger (as opposed to unhealthy anger)	Assertion
Healthy jealousy (as opposed to unhealthy jealousy)	Brief, open-minded questioning of the other person; neither checking on the other nor restricting them
Healthy envy (as opposed to unhealthy envy)	Striving to gain a similar possession for oneself if it is truly what you want

Realistic Thinking Associated with HNEs

As I have pointed out, when you experience an HNE, your associated thinking is likely to be realistic. There are certain forms of thinking that are frequently associated with particular HNEs. I provide a representative list below. This should be compared with the list of distorted thinking associated with UNEs that I presented in chapter 20.

You should consult the list below if you need help in identifying thinking goals.

HNE	Realistic Thinking
Concern (as opposed to anxiety)	Realistically appraising the negative consequences of the threat if it occurs
Sadness (as opposed to depression)	Viewing the future with hope; seeing self as able to cope with adversity
Remorse (as opposed to guilt)	Assigning appropriate level of responsibility to self and to others
Disappointment (as opposed to shame)	Realistically appraising others' reactions to self and the extent of these reactions
Sorrow (as opposed to hurt)	Not thinking that the other has to put things right of their own accord; thinking that one can initiate the healing process oneself
Healthy anger (as opposed to unhealthy anger)	Only thinking that the other has malicious intent when there is clear evidence of this; thoughts of assertion rather than of exacting revenge
Healthy jealousy (as opposed to unhealthy jealousy)	Tending to see threats to one's relationship only when there is clear evidence that such threats exist
Healthy envy (as opposed to unhealthy envy)	Honestly admitting to oneself that one wants the desired possession for its own sake and not because the other person has it

23

Identify Your Beliefs

Earlier, I discussed the four main irrational beliefs - demands, awfulising beliefs, low frustration tolerance (LFT) beliefs and depreciation beliefs - and their rational alternatives - non-dogmatic preferences, anti-awfulising beliefs, high frustration tolerance (HFT) beliefs and acceptance beliefs. I suggest that you re-read this material in Section I in Part 1 of this book if you need to refresh your memory of these beliefs.

At this stage of the process, you are ready to identify your irrational beliefs about "A" that largely determined your unhealthy responses at "C". You are also ready to identify the rational alternatives to these irrational beliefs that will help you to achieve your emotional, behavioural and thinking goals when facing the "A" again.

While you will want to identify all the relevant irrational beliefs that are related to your emotional problem as this becomes manifest in specific situations (and, of course the rational alternatives to these irrational beliefs), you might find the following rules of thumb useful:

- When your emotional problem relates to lowered self-esteem, identify your demand and self-depreciation belief (and your alternative non-dogmatic preference and self-acceptance belief).
- When your emotional problem relates to unhealthy anger towards another person, identify your demand and other-depreciation belief (and your alternative non-dogmatic preference and other-acceptance belief).
- For all other problems, identify your demand and one of the following irrational beliefs: awfulising, LFT and depreciation of life conditions. In formulating the rational alternatives to these beliefs, identify your non-dogmatic preference and one of the following rational beliefs: anti-awfulising, HFT and acceptance of life conditions.

In formulating your rational beliefs, it is important that you realise that they are comprised of a number of components as shown below:

Non-dogmatic preference (e.g. *"I want Peter to like me, but he doesn't have to do so"*)

i) "asserted preference" component (e.g. *"I want Peter to like me . . ."*)
ii) "negated demand" component (e.g. *". . . but he doesn't have to do so"*)

Anti-awfulising belief (e.g. *"It's bad if Peter doesn't like me, but it isn't awful"*)

i) "asserted badness" component (e.g. *"It's bad if Peter doesn't like me . . .*)

ii) "negated awfulising" component (e.g. ". . . but it isn't awful")

HFT belief (e.g. *"If Peter doesn't like me, it would be hard to bear, but I could bear it and it would be worth it to me to do so"*)

i) "asserted struggle" component (e.g. *"If Peter doesn't like me, it would be hard to bear . . ."*)
ii) "negated unbearability" component (e.g. *". . . but I could bear it . . ."*)
iii) "worth bearing" component (e.g. *". . . and it would be worth it to me to do so"*)

Acceptance belief (e.g. *"If Peter doesn't like me, that would be bad, but it wouldn't mean that I am worthless. I am still the same acceptable human being whether Peter likes me or not"*)

i) "evaluation of a part of self or what has happened to self" component (e.g. *"If Peter doesn't like me that would be bad . . ."*)
ii) "negated self-depreciation" component (e.g. *". . . but it wouldn't mean that I am worthless . . ."*)
iii) "asserted self-acceptance" component (e.g *"I am still the same acceptable human being whether Peter likes me or not"*)

Here is Gina's ABC updated with her irrational and rational beliefs. This ABC contains her combined irrational belief (demand and self-depreciation belief) and rational alternatives. Later on, I detail her four irrational beliefs and rational alternatives and use these to show you how to question both sets of beliefs.

"Situation" = My friend told me that she saw my boyfriend eating with another woman

"A" = He will probably want to end our relationship

"iB" (Irrational belief) = He must not want to end our relationship. If he does, it means that I am unlovable	"rB" (Rational belief) = I don't want my boyfriend to want to end our relationship but this does not mean that he must not have this desire. If he does this would be bad, but does not mean that I am unlovable. My lovability is based on my being an unrateable, unique human being, not on him wanting have a relationship with me
"C" (Emotional) = Anxiety	"C" (Emotional goal) = Concern
(Behavioural) = Constantly phoning boyfriend for reassurance that he loves me	(Behavioural goal) = Ask boyfriend about the identity of the woman he ate out with and the nature of the relationship and assess his answer logically
(Thinking) = Thinking of boyfriend making love with the other woman	(Thinking goal) = Consider the best way of raising the issue with boyfriend

24

Review, and The Importance of Practising Your ABCs

Let me review what I have covered so far in Part 2 of this book. I introduced the ABC model that you can use when analysing specific examples of your target problems and discussed the following steps:

1   Write down a brief, objective description of the "situation" you were in.
2   Identify your "C" - your major disturbed emotion, your dysfunctional behaviour and your subsequent distorted thinking.
3   Identify your "A" - this is what you were most disturbed about in the situation.
    (Steps 2 and 3 are interchangeable)
4   Set emotional, behavioural and thinking goals.
5   Identify your irrational beliefs at "B" that underpin your disturbed reactions at "C" and the rational alternatives that will help you to achieve your goals.

You are advised to practise doing ABCs many times until the process begins to be familiar to you. Formally such practice in REBT is known as homework assignments and I will discuss this further later. Do not expect learning this skill to be easy at first. You are learning a new skill, and like any new skill it takes practice and hard work. If you are working with an REBT therapist, he or she will be very experienced in this process and will help you to learn to do it even when the problems you are facing are complex. So, show your therapist your completed ABCs and he or she will help you to correct your errors and thus improve your assessment skills.

25

Identify any
Meta-emotional Problems

So far I have presented the ABCs as if they are simple and straightforward, and sometimes they are exactly that. However, ABCs can also be more complicated. Essentially, the main factor that complicates ABCs is that people quite often give themselves emotional problems about their emotional problems. For instance, you may feel depressed about feeling anxious or guilty about losing your temper. These emotions are called meta-emotions in REBT and if they represent emotional problems, they are known as meta-emotional problems.

Let me go back to the example I introduced in Chapter 22 and I will show you what I mean.

"Situation" = *My friend told me that she saw my boyfriend eating with another woman*

"A1" = *He will probably want to end our relationship*

"iB1" (Irrational belief) = *He must not want to end this relationship. It will be awful if he does*

"C1" (Emotional) = *Anxiety*

(Behavioural) = *Constantly phoning boyfriend for reassurance that he still loves me*

(Thinking) = *Thinking of boyfriend making love with the other woman*

If Gina gives herself a meta-emotional problem – and it may be, for example, shame – this is what happens (to keep this simple, I will only consider the emotional C here).

a) The emotional part of "C1" becomes the new "situation" ("Situation 2" = *I feel anxious*)

b) "A2" is what Gina is most ashamed about in this situation ("A2" = *Being anxious is a weakness*)

c) This "A2" then triggers a new irrational belief ("iB2") = *I must not be weak and if I am it proves that I am a weak person*

d) This new irrational belief creates a new emotional "C" ("C2"), in this case shame ("C2" = *Shame*)

Meta-emotional problems are handled in just the same way as primary ABCs. In this case Gina's goal with respect to her shame would be to feel disappointed about having a weakness rather than ashamed and to identify the rational belief to help her to achieve this goal.

If you have a meta-emotional problem, you can choose which problem to work on first. If your meta-emotional problem gets in the way of dealing with your primary problem, it is best to deal with the meta-emotional problem first.

V

Question Your Irrational and Rational Beliefs

So far, I have helped you to select a specific example of your target problem, to assess this example using the ABC framework and to set appropriate feeling, behavioural and thinking goals for dealing constructively with the situation if confronted with it again. I have also helped you to see that your rational beliefs will help you to achieve these goals and that your irrational beliefs will lead to your UNE, dysfunctional behaviour and distorted subsequent thinking. You are now ready to question both your irrational and rational beliefs. The purpose of this questioning process is to help you see that your irrational beliefs *are* irrational (meaning inconsistent with reality, illogical and leading largely to unhealthy results) and that your rational beliefs *are* rational (meaning consistent with reality, logical and leading largely to healthy results). Having conviction in these rational beliefs comes later. In the chapters that follow, I will mainly concentrate on helping you to question your specific irrational beliefs and their rational alternatives. However, everything I discuss also applies to the questioning of core irrational beliefs (general irrational beliefs that are at the core of a number of your problems) and their rational alternatives (see Chapter 38).

There are a number of ways in which you can question your irrational and rational beliefs. For example, you can question your irrational beliefs first and then your rational beliefs, or you can question them at the same time. It is this latter approach that I will demonstrate here. If you are working with your combined irrational belief (i.e. a demand and one other irrational belief) what you do is take each component of this combined irrational belief and its rational alternative and ask yourself three questions:

1   Which of these component beliefs is true (or consistent with reality) and which is false (or inconsistent with reality)?
2   Which of these component beliefs is logical and which is illogical?
3   Which of these component beliefs will lead to largely healthy results and which to largely unhealthy results?

In each of your responses, you also give reasons for your answers.

Here, I will show you how Gina questioned each of her four irrational beliefs and their four rational alternatives so that you can see how to question each of yours. When you question your beliefs, you can question all four beliefs, but more often you will only question your combined beliefs (i.e. demand + other major irrational belief and non-dogmatic preference + other major rational alternative), as I explained earlier in Chapter 23.

26

Question Your Demands and Non-dogmatic Preferences

Gina's demand (see left) and her non-dogmatic preference (see right) appear below. Let's see how she questioned them.

My boyfriend must not want to end our relationship

I don't want my boyfriend to want to end our relationship, but this does not mean that he must not have this desire

> Which of these beliefs is true (or consistent with reality) and which is false (or inconsistent with reality)? Give reasons for your answer.

My non-dogmatic preference is true and my demand is false. While I can prove that I really don't want my boyfriend to end our relationship because I care for him and want him to reciprocate my feelings, and want our relationship to continue, it is also true that there is no law decreeing that this must not happen. If there were, it would be impossible for my boyfriend to want to end our relationship and sadly this is just not the case.

My demand is illogical while my non-dogmatic preference is logical. My demand is based on the same desire as my non-dogmatic preference, but this is transformed as we can see: *I don't want my boyfriend to want to end our relationship and therefore this absolutely must not happen.* Thus, it has two components. The first (*I really don't want my boyfriend to want to end our relationship*) is not rigid, but the second (*and therefore this must not happen*) is rigid. As such my rigid demand isn't logical since in logic one cannot derive something rigid from something that is not rigid. On the other hand, my non-dogmatic preference is logical since both parts are not rigid and thus the second component logically follows from the first. This can be clearly shown in Figure 1.

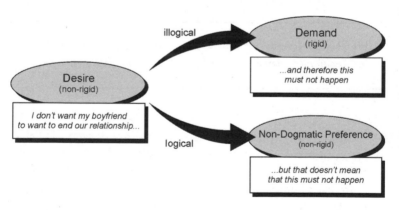

Figure 1 Why Gina's demand is illogical and her non-dogmatic preference is logical

dealing with emotional problems

My demand will lead largely to unhealthy results, while my non-dogmatic preference will lead to healthy results. My demand will lead me to feel anxious about being around my boyfriend and lead me to seek ongoing reassurance from him that he still loves me. I will also feel anxious when I am not with him since I will think that he will be making love with the woman that my friend saw him with the other night. My non-dogmatic preference, on the other hand, will lead me to feel concerned and help me to concentrate on what my boyfriend and I are doing when we are together and what I am doing when we are apart. It will also help me to ask him about the identity of the other woman so that I can determine whether or not she is a threat to our relationship.

27

Question Your Awfulising Beliefs and Anti-awfulising Beliefs

Gina's awfulising belief (see left) and her anti-awfulising belief (see right) appear below.

It would be terrible if my boyfriend wants to end our relationship

It would be very bad if my boyfriend wants to end our relationship, but it wouldn't be terrible

Which of these beliefs is true (or consistent with reality) and which is false (or inconsistent with reality)? Give reasons for your answer.

My anti-awfulising belief is true and my awfulising belief is false. While I can prove that it would be really bad if my boyfriend wanted to end our relationship since I love him and I want him to want me, it is also true that it is not terrible if this does happen. After all, some good might come of this bad situation as I can see that nothing is absolutely necessary for my happiness and that I can be happier with someone whom I love who wants me than with someone whom I love who doesn't want me.

> Which of these beliefs is logical and which is illogical? Give reasons for your answer.

My awfulising belief is illogical, while my anti-awfulising belief is logical. My awfulising belief is based on the same evaluation of badness as my anti-awfulising belief, but this is transformed as we can see: *It would be very bad if my boyfriend wanted to end our relationship and therefore it would be terrible.* Thus, it has two components. The first (*It would be very bad if my boyfriend wanted to end our relationship*) is non-extreme, while the second (*and therefore it would be terrible*) is extreme. As such my awfulising belief is illogical since in logic one cannot derive something extreme from something that is not extreme. On the other hand, my anti-awfulising belief is logical since both parts are non-extreme and thus the second component logically follows from the first. This can be clearly shown in Figure 2.

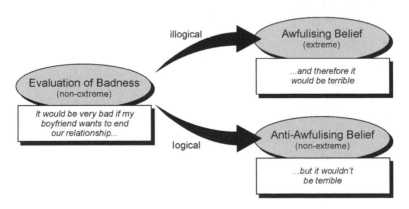

Figure 2 Why Gina's awfulising belief is illogical and her anti-awfulising belief is logical

My awfulising belief will lead largely to unhealthy results, while my anti-awfulising belief will lead to healthy results. My awfulising belief, like my rigid demand, will lead me to feel anxious about my boyfriend's intentions and will lead me to ask him constantly about his feelings for me, which may in itself affect our relationship negatively. It will lead me to think about my boyfriend making love with the other woman and also stop me from thinking about how to best raise the issue about her identity. My anti-awfulising belief, on the other hand, like my non-dogmatic preference, will lead me to feel concerned and help me to concentrate on our relationship when I am with my boyfriend and on other issues when I am not. It will also help me to see that there may be both good and bad consequences of my boyfriend wanting to end our relationship since while I would like him to want our relationship to continue, I can also see that it is bad to be with someone who doesn't want to be with me.

28

Question Your LFT and HFT Beliefs

Gina's LFT belief (see left) and her HFT belief (see right) appear below.

I wouldn't be able to tolerate it if my boyfriend wanted to end our relationship

It would be difficult for me to tolerate my boyfriend wanting to end our relationship, but I could tolerate it and it would be worth it to me to do so

> Which of these beliefs is true (or consistent with reality) and which is false (or inconsistent with reality)? Give reasons for your answer.

My HFT belief is true and my LFT belief is false. I can prove that it would be difficult for me to tolerate my boyfriend wanting to end our relationship since it would have a number of very bad consequences for me and I can also prove that I could tolerate it. If it were intolerable, I would either die, disintegrate or lose my capacity for happiness. This means that if my boyfriend did want to end our relationship, I would be unable to enjoy being with my friends or doing my job which

I love. This is obviously untrue. I can also prove that it is worth it to me to put up with my boyfriend wanting to end our relationship since as I have said before some good things could definitely come from this very unfortunate event.

> Which of these beliefs is logical and which is illogical? Give reasons for your answer.

My LFT belief is illogical, while my HFT belief is logical. My LFT belief is based on the same idea of struggle as my HFT belief, namely that my boyfriend wanting to end our relationship is difficult to tolerate, but this is transformed as we can see: *It would be difficult for me to tolerate my boyfriend wanting to end our relationship and therefore it would be intolerable.* Thus, it has two components. The first (*It would be difficult for me to tolerate my boyfriend wanting to end our relationship*) is non-extreme, while the second (*and therefore it would be intolerable*) is extreme. As such my LFT is illogical since in logic one cannot derive something extreme from something that is not extreme. On the other hand, my HFT belief is logical since both parts are non-extreme and thus the second component logically follows from the first. This can be clearly shown in Figure 3.

> Which of these beliefs will lead to largely healthy results and which to largely unhealthy results?

My LFT belief will lead largely to unhealthy results, while my HFT belief will largely lead to healthy results. My LFT belief,

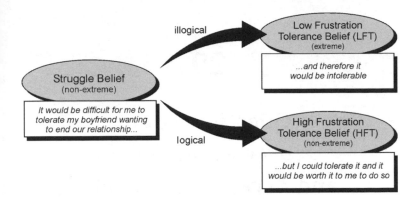

Figure 3 Why Gina's LFT belief is illogical and her HFT belief is logical

like my demand and my awfulising belief, will lead me to feel anxious about my boyfriend's feelings for me and will lead me to constantly seek reassurance that he still cares for me when I am with him. It will also lead to my fantasising about him making love to this other woman when I am not with him. My HFT belief, on the other hand, like my non-dogmatic preference and my anti-awfulising belief will lead me to feel concerned and help me to concentrate on what I am doing when I am not with my boyfriend and to enjoy our time together when I am with him. It will also lead me to ask him in a non-threatening way about the identity of the woman in question.

29

Question Your Depreciation Beliefs and Acceptance Beliefs

Gina's self-depreciation belief (see left) and her self-acceptance belief (see right) appear below.

If my boyfriend wants to end our relationship, it means that I am unlovable

If my boyfriend wants to end our relationship that would be bad, but it does not mean that I am unlovable. My lovability is based on me being an unrateable, unique human being and not on him wanting to have a relationship with me

Which of these beliefs is true (or consistent with reality) and which is false (or inconsistent with reality)? Give reasons for your answer.

My self-acceptance belief is true and my self-depreciation belief is false. I can prove that it is bad if my boyfriend wants to end our relationship since once again I love him and I want him to want me, and I can also prove that I am an unrateable, unique human being whose lovability is based on these unchangeable features. If I were unlovable then everything about me would be unlovable. This is obviously untrue.

Which of these beliefs is logical and which is illogical? Give reasons for your answer.

My self-depreciation belief is illogical, while my self-acceptance belief is logical. My self-depreciation belief is based on the same idea as in my self-acceptance belief that my boyfriend wanting to end our relationship is bad, but this is transformed as we can see: *My boyfriend wanting to end our relationship is bad and therefore I am unlovable.* Thus, it has two components. The first (*My boyfriend wanting to end our relationship is bad*) is an evaluation of a part of my experience, while the second (*and therefore I am unlovable*) is an evaluation of the whole of my "self". As such, I am making the illogical part-whole error where the part is deemed to define the whole. On the other hand, my self-acceptance is logical because it shows that my "self" is complex and incorporates a bad event such as my boyfriend wanting to end our relationship. Thus, my self-acceptance belief avoids the part-whole error.

Which of these beliefs will lead to largely healthy results and which to largely unhealthy results?

My self-depreciation belief will lead largely to unhealthy results, while my self-acceptance belief will lead to healthy results. My self-depreciation belief, like my demand, my awfulising belief and my LFT belief, will lead me to feel anxious about losing my boyfriend and to seek his constant reassurance that he loves me. It will also lead me to think about him having sex with the woman he was seen eating with. My self-acceptance belief, on the other hand, like my non-dogmatic preference, my anti-awfulising belief and my HFT belief, will lead me to feel concerned about our relationship and to ask my boyfriend about the identity of the other woman. It will also help me to focus on what I am doing when I am not with my boyfriend rather than thinking about him having sex with the other woman.

In the next step, I will outline a number of other ways in which you can dispute your irrational beliefs.

30

Variations on a Theme

What I have just presented is a structured approach to questioning irrational and rational beliefs. I suggest that you begin by using such a structure before using a more free-form approach to questioning beliefs. This is a bit like jazz, where you are encouraged to practise the basics of a song before improvising on its theme.

FREE-FORM QUESTIONING

Free-form questioning incorporates the "is it true?", "is it logical?", "is it healthy?" arguments, but in a free-form way. Here you are encouraged to use arguments that are particularly persuasive to you in whatever order you desire. The emphasis here is on persuasiveness rather than on comprehensiveness. Thus, if you don't use logical arguments, for example, in your questioning this is less important than the persuasiveness of the arguments that you do use. Here is an example of free-form questioning where Sally has identified a specific combined irrational belief (see left) and rational belief (see right) as shown below. Free-form questioning can also be used to question general or core irrational and rational beliefs.

I must not shake when I give the presentation this morning and if I do, it will be terrible	I don't want to shake when I give the presentation this morning, but that does not mean that I must not do so. If I do, that would be bad, but not terrible

SALLY'S QUESTIONING

I really don't want to shake when I give the presentation this morning because I want to make a good impression, but it doesn't follow that I have to be completely steady. My best bet is to concentrate on what I intend to say than on trying to control my shakiness. I know that when I demand that I don't shake then I will increase the chances that I will shake since this belief will make me anxious. But, if I shake in proportion and show myself that if I shake that would be unfortunate, but hardly terrible, then I will be concerned but not anxious about not appearing steady. This will help me to focus on what I have to say rather than on impressing people. I can prove that shaking isn't terrible since I can think of many, many things that are worse. So I will remind myself that if I shake, I shake - too bad.

LETTER TO A LOVED ONE

This technique is best used as a way of questioning core irrational and rational beliefs (see Chapter 38), although it can also be used to question specific beliefs. Once you have identified your core irrational belief and its rational alternative, you choose a loved one to write a letter to, the purpose of which is to teach the person a healthy way of living. Then, you ask yourself if there is any obstacle that would stop you from adopting this core belief for yourself. If there is any such obstacle, then you deal with it.

dealing with emotional problems

Here is an example of how Malcolm used this variation on the belief questioning theme. Malcolm's core irrational belief (see left) and rational alternative (see right) are presented below.

I must be successful and if I'm not, I am a nobody

I'd like to be successful, but this isn't essential for me. I'm important whether I am successful or not

Malcolm decided to write this letter to his newly-born son, Harry.

Dear Harry,

As you grow up, you will be faced with a number of things to do at school, at college if you go, or at work. Being successful at what you do is important for a number of reasons. It will give you satisfaction in and of itself, but it will help to get you a more comfortable life materially. However, no matter how important being successful is, Harry, I want you to realise that it isn't everything in life. There is your own family should you have one, a life partner, your friends and your mother and I who will love you no matter how well or poorly you do in life. Thus, it is important for you not to base your identity on being successful. If you do, you will be depressed and desperate if you are not successful and you will be anxious about later failure if you are successful. On the other hand, regarding yourself as important whether you are successful or not will lead you to deal with the pain of failure in healthy ways. Thus, you will feel sad rather than being depressed about failure. When you are successful, this healthy belief will enable you to relax and enjoy it, rather than being anxious about failing later. It will also help you to learn from any failures that you experience in life.

So, Harry, do your best in life. Enjoy your successes and learn from your failures. But whatever happens regard yourself as important and challenge any notion that if you are not successful then you are a nobody.

Love,
Dad

Once he had written this, Malcolm asked himself what would stop him from implementing the same advice in his own life. He decided that the only obstacle was: *Believing that the idea: "I must be successful or I am a nobody" motivates me to succeed in life and without it I wouldn't try to do well in life.* He responded to this obstacle in the following way: *The healthy motivation to be successful lies in my strong desire to succeed, not in my rigid and extreme idea that I must succeed and I am a nobody if I don't. This latter idea may motivate me temporarily, but it will also lead to emotional disturbance which will hold me back in life.*

31

The Importance of Practising
Your Disputing Skills

I mentioned in Chapter 24 that it is important for you to
carry out regular ABCs as homework assignments in order to
develop your skill at assessing specific examples of your target
problems. The same principle applies to questioning beliefs.
Regularly use one or more of the techniques that I have
described in the previous chapters to develop your questioning skills. Then, show this homework to your REBT therapist
(if you are consulting one) and he or she will help you to
correct your errors and improve your disputing or questioning skills.

The purpose of the questioning process is to help you
understand that your irrational beliefs are irrational and your
rational beliefs are rational. What I have covered so far applies
to questioning your specific beliefs and your core beliefs.
Developing true conviction in your rational beliefs (specific
and core) so that you believe them in your gut as well as
understand them in your head is the subject of Chapters
32-36.

VI

Strengthen Your Conviction in Your Rational Beliefs

In the following five chapters, I will teach you a number of techniques devised to help you strengthen your conviction in your rational beliefs and weaken your conviction in your irrational beliefs. Unfortunately, you need to work at truly believing rational beliefs in the sense that they make a real difference to the way that you feel and how you act. Why? Because just understanding that your rational beliefs are consistent with reality, and are logical and helpful to you is not sufficient to bring about change. This form of under-standing is known as "intellectual insight" and when you have it you say things such as "I understand why my rational belief is rational, but I don't believe it yet" or "I understand that my rational belief is rational up here" (referring to your head) "but not down here" (referring to your gut). Intellectual insight is necessary to help you change your core and specific rational beliefs but it is not sufficient for you to do so.

The type of insight that does promote change is known by REBT therapists as "emotional insight". If you have this type of insight you would say such things as "Not only do I believe it in my head, I feel it in my gut" and "I really believe in my heart that my rational belief is true, logical and helpful." The true indicator of whether you have emotional insight into your specific and core rational beliefs is that these beliefs lead to healthy emotions, functional behaviour and realistic, balanced subsequent thinking. In the following chapters, I will describe a number of techniques that are designed to help you to believe in your gut what you understand in your head. My aim is to be illustrative, rather than comprehensive, in outlining such techniques. Your REBT therapist (if you are consulting one) will suggest a range of such techniques based on your own unique set of circumstances. You might want to have a look at Dryden (2001) for more details about such techniques.

32

Use the Attack-response Technique

This technique, which is sometimes called the zig-zag technique, is based on the idea that you can strengthen your conviction in a rational belief by responding persuasively to attacks on this belief. I will outline the main (written) version of the attack-response technique, but there are also several variations on the same theme described more fully in Dryden (2001).

HOW TO COMPLETE A WRITTEN ATTACK-RESPONSE FORM

1 Write down your specific (or core) rational belief on a piece of paper.
2 Rate your present level of conviction in this belief on a 100% point scale with 0% = no conviction and 100% = total conviction (i.e. I really believe this in my gut and it markedly influences my feelings and behaviour). Write down this rating under your belief.
3 Write down an attack on this rational belief. Your attack may take the form of a doubt, reservation or objection to this rational belief. It should also contain an explicit irrational belief (e.g. demand, awfulising belief, LFT belief

or depreciating belief). Make this attack as genuine as you can. The more it reflects what you believe, the better.

4   Respond to this attack as fully as you can. It is really important that you respond to each element of the attack. In particular, make sure that you respond to irrational belief statements and also to distorted or unrealistic inferences framed in the form of a doubt, reservation or objection to the rational belief. Do so as persuasively as possible and write down your response.

5   Continue in this vein until you have answered all of your attacks and cannot think of any more. Make sure throughout this process that you are keeping the focus on the rational belief that you are trying to strengthen. If you find this exercise difficult, you might find it easier to make your attacks gently at first. Then, when you find that you can respond to these attacks quite easily, begin to make the attacks more biting. Work in this way until you are making really strong attacks. When you make an attack, do so as if you really want to believe it. And when you respond, really throw yourself into it with the intention of demolishing the attack and of strengthening your conviction in your rational belief. Don't forget that the purpose of this exercise is to strengthen your conviction in your rational belief, so it is important that you stop only when you have answered all of your attacks. If you make an attack that you cannot respond to, stop the exercise and raise the matter with your REBT therapist or consult one for help with this issue.

6   When you have answered all of your attacks, re-rate your level of conviction in your rational belief using the 0–100% scale as before. If you have succeeded in responding persuasively to your attacks, then this rating will have gone up appreciably. If it has not increased or it has only done so a little, discuss this with an REBT therapist.

Here is how Gina used the attack-response technique:

Rational belief: I don't want my boyfriend to want to end our relationship, but this does not mean that he must not have this desire. If he does this is bad, but it does not mean that I am unlovable. My lovability is based on my being an unrateable, unique human being, not on my boyfriend wanting to have a relationship with me.
Conviction rating of rational belief = 35%

Attack: But I have known him for ages. If he wants to break up with me, it must mean that he sees that I am flawed as a person. If he does this proves that I am unlovable.

Response: If he does want to break up with me, it does not necessarily mean that he thinks that I am defective, but if he does, this does not make me defective or unlovable. My view of myself is not formed by his view of me. I can still accept myself even if my boyfriend thinks that I am defective

Attack: But he knows me very well. If he thinks that I am defective, he must be right.

Response: Yes he knows me very well, but it doesn't matter how well he knows me, if he thinks that I am defective, he is wrong. I may have some characteristics that are unfortunate or even defective if you will but that does not mean that I am defective as a person. I am not. I am a unique, fallible human who has good, bad and neutral characteristics.

Attack: But if my boyfriend does prefer the woman my friend saw him with, it means that I am less lovable than she is.

Response: No, it doesn't. It means that at this time he would rather go out with her than me. If this is the case, I will be very sad about this, but I refuse to tie my worth into it. I am not less worthy than the other woman. We are of equal worth because we are both human. This is true whether my boyfriend wants me rather than her or vice versa.

Conviction rating of original rational belief = 75%

I mentioned earlier that there are a number of variations of the attack-response technique. You can tape-record the dialogue and make sure that your response is more forceful in tone and language than your attack. You can also use the technique with your therapist who will make increasingly biting attacks on your rational belief, encouraging you to respond effectively to these attacks. This is often called "devil's advocate disputing" by REBT therapists.

33

Use Rational-emotive Imagery

Rational-emotive imagery (REI) is an imagery method designed to help you practise changing your *specific* irrational belief to its healthy equivalent while you imagine, at the same time, focusing on what you are most disturbed about in a *specific* situation in which you felt disturbed. Because you can only use REI while imagining specific situations, it is recommended for use only to strengthen your conviction in *specific* rational beliefs. There are two versions of REI, one devised by Dr Albert Ellis, the originator of REBT, and the other devised by Dr Maxie C. Maultsby Jr. I will teach you the Ellis version here. If needs be your therapist will teach you the Maultsby version.

REI is based on the fact that you can use your imagery modality to help you get over your problems or, albeit unwittingly, to practise thinking unhealthily as you imagine a host of negative situations about which you disturb yourself. In the latter case, when you think about a negative event and you disturb yourself about it, you are likely to do so by imagining the event in your mind's eye and covertly rehearsing one or more irrational beliefs about the event. In this way, you literally practise disturbing yourself and at the same time you end up strengthening your conviction in your irrational beliefs.

Fortunately, you can also use your mind's eye for constructive purposes. For instance, while imagining the same negative event as above, you can practise changing your UNEs to their healthy equivalents by changing your specific irrational beliefs to specific rational beliefs.

What follows is a set of instructions for using Ellis's version of REI.

INSTRUCTIONS FOR USING REI: ELLIS VERSION

1   Take a situation in which you disturbed yourself and identify the aspect of the situation you were most disturbed about.

2   Close your eyes and imagine the situation as vividly as possible and focus on the adversity at "A".

3   Allow yourself to really experience the UNE that you felt at the time while still focusing intently on the "A". Ensure that your UNE is *one* of the following: anxiety, depression, shame, guilt, hurt, unhealthy anger, unhealthy jealousy, unhealthy envy.

4   Really experience this disturbed emotion for a moment or two and then change your emotional response to an HNE, while all the time focusing intently on the adversity at "A". Do not change the intensity of the emotion, just the emotion. Thus, if your original UNE was anxiety, change this to concern; if it was depression, change it to sadness. Change shame to disappointment, guilt to remorse, hurt to sorrow, unhealthy anger to healthy anger, unhealthy jealousy to healthy jealousy and unhealthy envy to healthy envy. Again change the UNE to its healthy equivalent, but keep the level of intensity of the new emotion as strong as the old emotion. Keep experiencing this new emotion for about five minutes, all the time focusing on the adversity at "A". If you go back to the old UNE, bring the new HNE back.

5   At the end of five minutes, ask yourself how you changed
    your emotion.
6   Make sure that you changed your emotional response by
    changing your specific irrational belief to its healthy alter-
    native. If you did not do so (if, for example, you changed
    your emotion by changing the "A" to make it less negative
    or neutral or by holding an indifference belief about the
    "A"), do the exercise again and keep doing this until you
    have changed your emotion only by changing your specific
    unhealthy belief to its healthy alternative.

Discuss any problems that you have with using REI with your
therapist.

My final point about REI concerns how frequently you
should practise it. I suggest that you practise it several times
a day and aim for 30 minutes daily practice (when you are
not doing any other therapy homework). You might practise
it more frequently and for a longer period of time when you
are about to face a negative situation about which you are
likely to disturb yourself. When you are doing other therapy
homework, 15 minutes daily REI practice will suffice.

34

Teach Rational
Beliefs to Others

Another way of strengthening your conviction in your rational beliefs is to teach them to others. I am not suggesting that you play the role of therapist to friends and relatives nor am I suggesting that you foist these ideas on people who are not interested in discussing them. Rather, I am suggesting that you teach rational beliefs to people who hold the alternative irrational beliefs and are interested in hearing what you have to say on the subject. When you do this, and in particular when the other person argues with your viewpoint in defending their position, you get the experience of responding to their arguments with persuasive arguments of your own, and in doing so you strengthen your conviction in your own rational beliefs. I suggest that you do this after you have developed competence in using the written attack-response technique discussed earlier, since the back and forth discussion which often ensues when you attempt to teach rational beliefs to others is reminiscent of this technique.

35

Use Rational Self-statements

Once you have developed either specific or core rational beliefs, you can develop short-hand versions of these beliefs which you can write down on a small card or type into the message folder of your mobile phone for later periodic use. Such review is useful both when you are about to face an adversity and when you are actually facing one, assuming that it is feasible to glance at your rational message. You can also repeat these self-statements to yourself in a forceful, persuasive manner. When you review such rational self-statements focus on their meaning. Mindless repetition of these statements will have little or no impact on your feelings or behaviour.

Here are few examples of rational self-statements that my clients have used:

> ⟳ "I want to pass my driving test tomorrow, but I definitely don't have to do so."
>
> ⟳ "Failing my exam was a disadvantage, but does not prove that I am a failure. I am fallible and can retake the exam next year."
>
> ⟳ "It is not awful if my girlfriend rejects me, just very unfortunate."
>
> ⟳ "Feeling anxious is not unbearable, but it is a very unpleasant emotion. I can bear it and it is worth bearing."

36

Rehearse your Rational Beliefs while Acting and Thinking in Ways that are Consistent with these Beliefs

Perhaps the most powerful way of strengthening your target rational belief is to rehearse it while facing the relevant adversity at "A" and while acting and thinking in ways that are consistent with this rational belief. When your behaviour and thinking are in sync and you keep them in sync, you maximise your chances of strengthening your conviction in your target rational belief. Conversely, refrain from acting and thinking in ways that are consistent with your old irrational belief. It will be difficult for you to so refrain because you are used to acting and thinking in unconstructive ways when your specific (or core) irrational belief is activated. However, if you monitor your belief, your behaviour and your subsequent thinking, and respond constructively when you notice unhealthy instances, then you will gain valuable experience in strengthening your conviction in your rational belief.

As you work to strengthen your conviction in your target rational beliefs, bear in mind the following:

⊃ You may have been employing a number of safety-seeking strategies designed to help you avoid facing adversities or to help you stay safe if you have to face these adversities. Continued use of these strategies while you are endeavouring to change your irrational beliefs will ultimately mean that you will not change these beliefs. Identify your use of these strategies (which are largely behavioural and thinking in nature and can often be subtle and difficult to spot) and dispute the irrational beliefs that often underpin them so that you can face the adversities fairly and squarely while rehearsing your developing rational beliefs. Your REBT therapist, if you are consulting one, will also help you to do this.

⊃ You will only experience a change in your emotions (from negative and unhealthy to negative and healthy) after regular integrated practice where you rehearse your rational beliefs and act and think in ways that are consistent with these beliefs. Thus, emotional change tends to lag behind behavioural change and thinking change. If you understand this, then you will persist at changing your belief, behaviour and subsequent thinking and will not get discouraged when your feelings take a longer time to change.

⊃ It is also important that you face negative events about which you have a problem so that you can practise your rational beliefs and the realistic thinking and functional behaviour that stem from these beliefs. Thus, if you are endeavouring to practise your rational belief: "I don't want to be criticised by Paul, but I am not immune from such criticism. I am not a bad person for being criticised by Paul even if it is accurate. Rather, I am a fallible person whose worth is fixed and is not diminished by Paul's criticism, accurate or inaccurate", it is important that you review this belief in the face of criticism from Paul.

⊃ It is important that you expose yourself to events that pose a challenge to you, but which you do not find overwhelming at that time. To get the most out of such exposure, you need to do it regularly while rehearsing your target rational belief and thinking realistically. As you make progress, keep stretching yourself until you can face quite challenging events.

VII

Other Issues

37

Reconsider "A"

In Chapter 21 when I discussed identifying your "A" I encouraged you to assume temporarily that your "A" (i.e. the aspect of the situation that you were most disturbed about) was true. I urged you to do this because this is the best way for you to identify the unhealthy irrational beliefs that lie at the core of your disturbed reactions at "C" in the ABC framework. If you were to re-examine your "A" earlier in the emotional episode under consideration you may realise that your interpretation or inference of the situation was distorted and thus change it. While you might feel better as a result, you would not have gained practice at identifying, challenging and changing your irrational beliefs. Consequently, these beliefs would remain intact and would be triggered the next time you encountered a similar "A".

In addition, because your disturbed feelings stem largely from your irrational belief about "A" rather than from "A" itself, your attempts to reconsider this "A" while you hold an irrational belief about it will be coloured by this belief and any reconsideration of the distorted inference you may have made at "A" will probably be short-lived. Alternatively, once you have made progress at changing your irrational belief about "A", you are likely to be in a more objective frame of mind and it is this frame of mind that best facilitates accurate re-examination of "A".

So how do you go about re-examining "A"? By going back to it and asking yourself whether or not this was the most realistic way of looking at the situation. This does not mean that you can know for certain that your "A" was true or false for there is rarely any absolute and agreed correct way of viewing an event. What it does mean is that you can weigh up all the evidence that is available to you about the situation at hand and make what is likely to be the "best bet" about what happened.

I now list a number of ways of re-examining "A" to determine whether or not it was the most realistic way of viewing what happened in the situation in which you disturbed yourself. In doing so I will show what Gina did when she came to re-examine her "A".

Go back to your ABC and focus on what you wrote under the heading "situation". Then, ask yourself whether what you listed under "A" was the most realistic way of viewing the situation given all the evidence to hand. This involves considering the inference that you made that forms "A", considering alternative inferences, evaluating all the possibilities and choosing the most realistic inference.

Gina asked herself how likely it was that being seen eating with another woman meant that her boyfriend would probably want to end their relationship. In formulating an answer to this question, Gina considered the following:

1 Has my boyfriend indicated verbally that he is unhappy with our relationship? Answer: no. He tells me that he loves and cares for me quite often, sometimes without being prompted or asked.

2 Has my boyfriend's behaviour suggested that he wants to end our relationship. Answer: no. Our lovemaking is as frequent and passionate as ever. He calls me as frequently

as ever and although he has been tired recently, this is probably due to the fact that he is going through a very busy period at work.

3 Have I any other evidence in favour of my inference that my boyfriend wants to end our relationship? Answer: none that I can think of.

Gina then identified alternative explanations for her boyfriend eating out with another woman. She came up with the following:

1 My boyfriend was eating with a work colleague.
2 My boyfriend was eating with a female friend whom he does not find attractive.
3 My boyfriend was eating with a female friend whom he does find attractive, but is not interested in pursuing a romantic or sexual relationship with.
4 My boyfriend was eating with a female relative.

Finally, Gina reviewed the evidence concerning the likelihood of these alternative explanations. In doing so, she took into account her boyfriend's general behaviour in their relationship, her own tendency to be jealous and her friend's taste for generating gossip. After she answered her own questions and reviewed the other alternative explanations for her boyfriend eating out with another woman, Gina concluded, based on the evidence at hand, that her boyfriend was probably eating out with a work colleague. She then asked him about the identity of the woman concerned and it turned out that she was her boyfriend's second cousin whom he bumped into at lunch time and they went for a quick bite to eat.

However, what if Gina's boyfriend had indicated both verbally and behaviourally that he was unhappy with the state of their relationship and was considering breaking off with her? If this was the case when Gina came to re-examine her "A", she would likely decide that her "A" was the best bet of all the inferences she had identified (i.e. the fact that her boyfriend was seen eating with another woman meant he wanted to end his relationship with her). However, it could still have turned out that the other woman was a relative of his. Consequently, it is important to keep in mind that even your best bet at "A" may prove to be wrong. Consequently, it is important to test it out wherever possible *after* you have made yourself relatively undisturbed about your original inference at "A".

Other ways of re-examining "A" are as follows:

1 How likely is it that "A" happened (or might happen)?
2 Would an objective jury agree that "A" happened or might happen? If not, what would the jury's verdict be?
3 Did I view (am I viewing) the situation realistically? If not, how could I have viewed (can I view) it more realistically?
4 If I asked someone whom I could trust to give me an objective opinion about the truth or falsity of my inference about the situation at hand, what would the person say to me and why? How would this person encourage me to view the situation instead?
5 If a friend had told me that they had faced (were facing or were about to face) the same situation as I faced and had made the same inference, what would I say to him or her about the validity of their inference and why? How would I encourage the person to view the situation?

38

Identify and Deal with
Core Irrational Beliefs

As is apparent in its title, this book is designed to get you started using REBT with your emotional problems. As such I have mainly focused on helping you to deal with specific examples of the problems that you wish to tackle in therapy or on your own. I close this guide with some suggestions on how to identify and deal with core irrational beliefs. A full discussion of this topic is outside this book's brief, but can be found in the companion book (Dryden 2001). If you are consulting an REBT therapist then he or she will help you to work with your core irrational beliefs.

WHAT IS A CORE IRRATIONAL BELIEF AND ITS RATIONAL ALTERNATIVE?

A core irrational belief is a general irrational belief that underpins a number of your psychological problems. It usually has a specific theme and spans a number of situations where you disturb yourself. If it concerns other people it usually relates to a number of people. Like a specific irrational belief it comprises a demand and at least one of the other irrational beliefs listed earlier in this book (i.e. awfulising, LFT and/or depreciation beliefs).

The goal of working with a core irrational belief is to change it to a core rational belief. A core rational belief is also a general belief, but one that underpins your healthy responses to adversity. It has the same specific theme as your core irrational belief, spans the same situations and involves the same people as your core irrational belief. Like a specific rational belief it comprises a non-dogmatic preference and at least one of the other rational beliefs listed earlier in this book (i.e. anti-awfulising, HFT and/or acceptance beliefs).

HOW TO IDENTIFY A CORE IRRATIONAL BELIEF

Here I will suggest a number of ways of identifying core irrational beliefs.

1   Identify the theme of your core irrational belief. To do this you can look for a repeated theme in: your formulated problems; your written ABCs; your mental preoccupations; situations that you routinely avoid; your nightmare scenarios.
2   Specify relevant groups of situations and people.
3   Add the demand and at least one other relevant irrational belief.

Here are some examples of core irrational beliefs with the relevant theme in italics.

- ➲ "I must be *approved* by authority figures and if not, I am worthless"
- ➲ "I must be *certain* that my loved ones are safe and I can't bear not knowing this"
- ➲ "I must *succeed* at work and I am a failure if I don't"
- ➲ I must have *autonomy* in my relationships and it is awful when I don't"

HOW TO CHANGE A CORE IRRATIONAL BELIEF

Here are a number of suggestions of how to change core irrational beliefs.

1   Specify the rational alternative to the core irrational belief (i.e. the core rational belief).
2   Question your core irrational and rational beliefs using the methods outlined in Chapters 26-30.
3   Strengthen your conviction in your core rational beliefs using the following techniques: use the attack-response technique; teach rational beliefs to others; use rational self-statements.
4   Rehearse your rational beliefs while acting and thinking in ways that are consistent with these beliefs. Do this while approaching relevant situations, in a way that is challenging to you but not overwhelming at any point.

A Final Word

This is the end of this concise guide to getting started with REBT. If you want more detailed information about using REBT, I suggest that you consult my client workbook (Dryden 2001).

For those of you who want specific help with specific emotional problems the following reading may be useful:

Dryden, W. (1992) *The Incredible Sulk*. London: Sheldon Press.

Dryden, W. (1994) *Overcoming Guilt*. London: Sheldon Press.

Dryden, W. (1996) *Overcoming Anger: When Anger Helps and When It Hurts*. London: Sheldon Press.

Dryden, W. (1997) *Overcoming Shame*. London: Sheldon Press.

Dryden, W. (1998) *Overcoming Jealousy*. London: Sheldon Press.

Dryden, W. (2000) *Overcoming Procrastination*. London: Sheldon Press.

Dryden, W. (2000) *Overcoming Anxiety*. London: Sheldon Press.

Dryden, W. and Matweychuk, W. (2000) *Overcoming your Addictions*. London: Sheldon Press.

Dryden, W. (2002) *Overcoming Envy*. London: Sheldon Press.

Dryden, W. and Opie, S. (2003) *Overcoming Depression*. London: Sheldon Press.

For those of you who want books on more general issues, I recommend:

Dryden, W. and Gordon, J. (1993). *Beating the Comfort Trap*. London: Sheldon Press.

Dryden, W. (1999) *How to Accept Yourself*. London: Sheldon Press.

References

Beck, A.T. (1976) *Cognitive Therapy and the Emotional Disorders*. New York: International Universities Press.

Dryden, W. (2001) *Reason to Change: A Rational Emotive Behaviour Therapy (REBT) Workbook*. Hove: Brunner-Routledge.

Dryden, W. and Feltham, C. (1995) *Counselling and Psychotherapy: A Consumer's Guide*. London: Sheldon Press.

DATE DUE
